WHAT IS COMMUNISM?

Social Studies Book Grade 6

Children's Government Books

BABY PROFESSOR
EDUCATION KIDS

Speedy Publishing LLC

40 E. Main St. #1156

Newark, DE 19711

www.speedypublishing.com

Copyright 2017

Communism is a powerful economic and social idea that led to revolutions and great changes in many nations. Learn about the principles and notable people of the Communist movement.

WHAT COMMUNISM WANTS

Under an ideal communist system, nearly all property and wealth belongs to all the people, not to individuals. People do not work to get rich: they work to do what the country needs to become stronger, while the country provides what they need, from housing to healthcare to education, at little or no cost.

SYMBOL OF COMMUNISM

EGYPTIAN COMMUNIST PARTY
FLAGS IN TAHRIR SQUARE

No modern society has ever had a pure communist system, although many countries have tried to move in that direction.

The communist idea sprang from frustration and anger with the evils of the capitalist system of the nineteenth century. There were few restraints on a rich person becoming even richer, and few supports to help a person who was sick, needed help getting an education, or could not find a job. Most of the wealth of a country was in the hands of a very few families, while the great mass of people did not have enough to live on.

COMMUNIST PARTY OF THE RUSSIAN
FEDERATION ASSEMBLY

STATUE KARL MARX AND FRIEDRICH ENGELS

Many people felt there had to be a better way. Philosophers Karl Marx and Friedrich Engels developed a "Communist Manifesto" that they published in 1848. They had a vision of shared ownership of all land and the means of production, reduction of the power of the central government, and putting all people on the same economic footing. Communism was often summarized as "from each according to his abilities, and to each according to his needs."

ACHIEVING COMMUNISM

Movement leaders thought communism would take hold first in developed countries like Great Britain, because the workers were educated and well aware of the inequalities and cruelties in their society. However, the first Communist country appeared in Russia, which became the Soviet Union, after World War I.

CHINESE COMMUNIST FLAG

TSAR NIKOLAI II

Read more about this period in the Baby Professor book Tsar Nicholas II: Last Russian Tsar. There the people wanted an end to the repressive imperial regime, where most laborers were essentially slaves. They fought not so much for communism as against the old government, and in fact a democratic government replaced the imperial government before it was overthrown by forces committed to communism.

P.C.I.

No country yet has voted to become a Communist nation, although in countries from Italy to Nepal communist political parties have been part of, or even formed, the government.

REVOLUTION

very country that became part of the Communist world between 1900 and 1950 did so as a result of war or revolution.

SICKLE AND HAMMER THE
SYMBOLS OF COMMUNISM

THE IDEA AND THE REALITY

Because communist regimes have almost always come into power through military force, and almost always face opposition from within and from other countries, they have tended to stay in "emergency mode". This has meant delaying the move to a point where all wealth is held in common and the power of the central state reduces. Instead, communist nations have argued that the current emergency requires a "vanguard party" leading the nation, by force, if necessary.

M any people seized the possibilities for corruption in centralized governments. The leadership of the nation's government and

FLAG OF THE CHINESE COMMUNIST PARTY

Communist Party in many countries were able to shop in special stores and have holiday homes in special places where the rest of the people had no access.

RUSSIAN COMMUNIST LEADERS

ВЫШЕ ЗНАМЯ МАРКСА. Э

At its worst, the excesses of Communist Party leaders under communism in the Soviet Union, for example, were little different from the excesses of the rich and powerful under the Tsars before the revolution, or in any capitalist country.

ЕЛЬСА, ЛЕНИНА и СТАЛИН

COMMUNIST COUNTRIES

At one point, as much as one third of the population of the Earth lived under communist regimes. It sometimes seemed as though the march of communism was inevitable: on the one side, the opposing ideology, capitalism, would break apart under its own contradictions; on the other side, the power of the people would in theory force governments aside.

THE FLAG OF THE SOVIET UNION USSR

In practice, capitalism proved more flexible than had been thought, and has been able to reduce pressure for change by raising the standard of living of all but the poorest of its citizens. Communist countries are much better at providing services such as free education and free healthcare, but have not been able to improve standards of living dramatically.

GOVERNMENT BUILDING ON THE CENTRAL SQUARE OF KIM IL-SUNG OF PYONGYANG

Further, the countries of the world are much more tightly connected now by trade, the Internet, and fast communication. When the Soviet Union broke up, its former countries could choose their path rather than being compelled into communism. Most have moved into some sort of democratic politics and economic policies that are closer to capitalism than communism. The remaining communist countries are China, Cuba, Laos, North Korea, and Vietnam. Given the size of China, this still represents over 20 percent of the world's population.

T he former Communist countries (using their current names) include:

- Countries that were part of the Soviet Union: Armenia, Azerbaijan, Belarus, Estonia, Georgia, Kazakhstan, Kyrgystan, Latvia, Lithuania, Moldova, Russia, Tajikistan, Turkmenistan, Ukraine, and Uzbekistan.
- Countries in Europe that had Communist governments imposed after World War II: Albania, Bulgaria, Czech Republic, East Germany, Hungary, Poland, Romania, and Slovakia.

YEREVAN IS THE ECONOMIC AND CULTURAL CENTRE OF ARMENIA

➲ Countries formerly part of Yugoslavia: Bosnia and Herzegovina, Croatia, Macedonia, Montenegro, Serbia, and Slovenia.

ANGOLA NATIONAL ASSEMBLY BUILDING

➲ African nations: Angola, Benin, Democratic Republic of
the Congo, Ethiopia, Somalia, Eritrea, and Mozambique.

MAJOR COMMUNIST LEADERS

Here are some of the world's leaders who brought the concept of communism from an idea to a theory, and then put that theory into practice.

KARL MARX (1818–1883)

Marx was a German philosopher and writer. He developed the principles of communism in reaction to what he saw as the horrible practices of nineteenth century capitalism in industrial Europe.

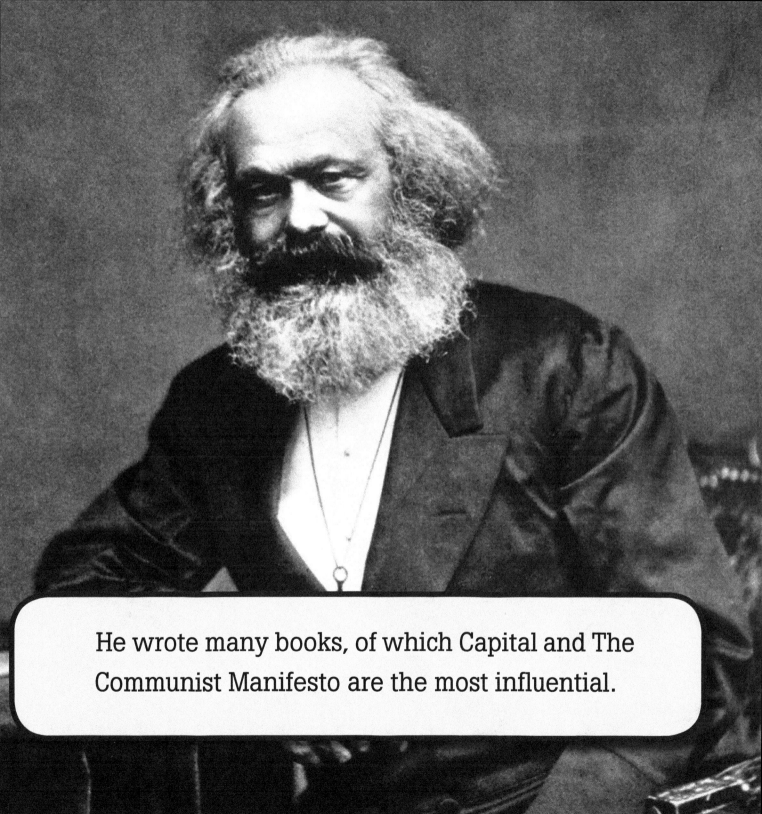

He wrote many books, of which Capital and The Communist Manifesto are the most influential.

VLADIMIR LENIN

VLADIMIR LENIN (1870-1924)

Lenin was one of the leaders of the Bolshevik movement in Russia and became head of the Soviet Union that emerged in Russia at the end of World War I. He strongly believed that the good of the workers depended on a strong "vanguard party" that would control central decisions. This allowed for modernization of the country, but led also to much sorrow.

JOSEF STALIN (1878-1953)

Stalin followed Lenin as leader of the Soviet Union and led it through the Great Depression, World War II, and the start of the Cold War.

MAO ZEDONG

MAO ZEDONG (1893-1976)

Mao led the People's Revolutionary Army in a long battle against other forces in China, and against Japanese invaders. When the Communists defeated the existing Chinese government in 1948, Mao became the head of the People's Republic of China. He led several upheavals in Chinese society, economics, and business, and made China a significant power on the world stage.

JOSIP TITO
(1892-1980)

Tito fought against Germany and Italy during World War II, helping the Balkan area regain its freedom from the Axis powers. (Learn more about this period in the Baby Professor book The Allied Powers vs. the Axis Powers in World War II.)

He became the president of Yugoslavia, a fragile coalition of seven regions that had been part of Austria-Hungary.

STEVAN KRAGUJEVIC, ELIZABETH II AND JOSIP BROZ TITO,1972

He was an excellent diplomat, and a practical leader in economic matters. Soon after his death, Yugoslavia separated, sometimes peacefully and sometimes after a war, into six countries.

HO CHI MINH (1890-1969)

Ho led Vietnam's fight for independence from 1941 until he defeated the French, who occupied Indo-China, in 1954. He then became president of North Vietnam. He led that country through a desperate war against South Vietnam, which was supported by the United States, dying in 1969 just before North Vietnam's victory and the reunification of Vietnam.

STATUE OF HO CHI MINH

KIM IL SUNG

KIM IL SUNG (1912–1994)

Kim Il Sung was the leader of North Korea from the founding of the country in 1948 until his death in 1994. He directed its attempt to conquer South Korea in the Korean War, 1951–53, and in the continuing war of nerves between the two countries over the following decades.

FIDEL CASTRO (1926–2016)

Castro launched a revolution against the dictatorial government of Cuba led by Fulgencio Batista, forming the Republic of Cuba in 1959. This was the first Communist country in the Americas.

Under Castro, Cuba made great advances in healthcare and education, but was constantly in conflict with the United States and its allies.

MIKHAIL GORBACHEV

MIKHAIL GORBACHEV
(BORN 1931)

Gorbachev was the last leader of the Soviet Union, from 1985 to 1991. He led the country through radical changes to its economy, system of government, and dictatorial style, changes known as "perestroika" (reorganization) and "glasnost" (opening up). He resolved a dispute with the United States over nuclear weapons, reducing world tensions and the risk of another world war.

THE DEVIL IS IN THE DETAILS

Countries have experienced a wide range of government systems, from the rule of kings to military dictatorships, from extreme capitalism to extreme communism. Some countries have a heavy emphasis on local decision-making, and some on extreme central control.

No one system has yet gotten everything right. No country yet has managed to experience economic prosperity, peace, environmental care, and well-being of all of its people, all at one time! This is much harder than it seems that it ought to be.

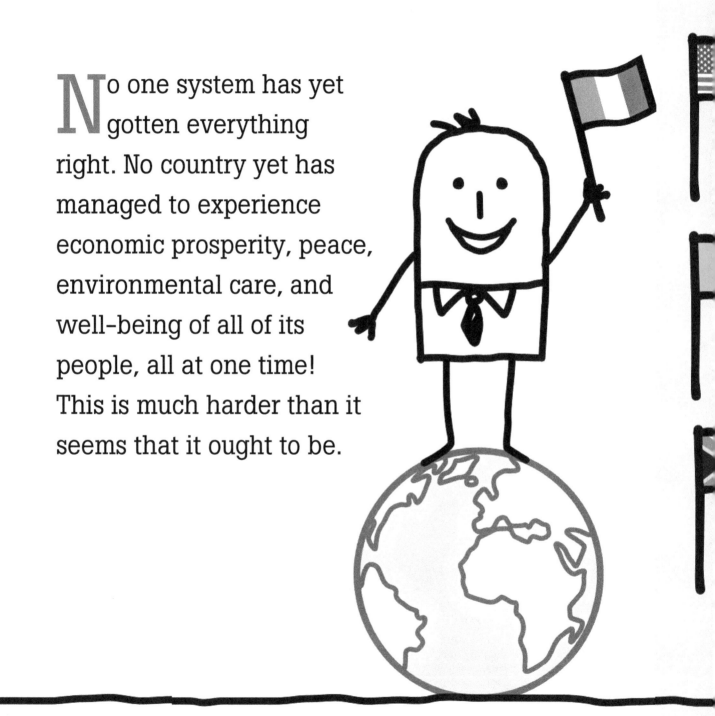

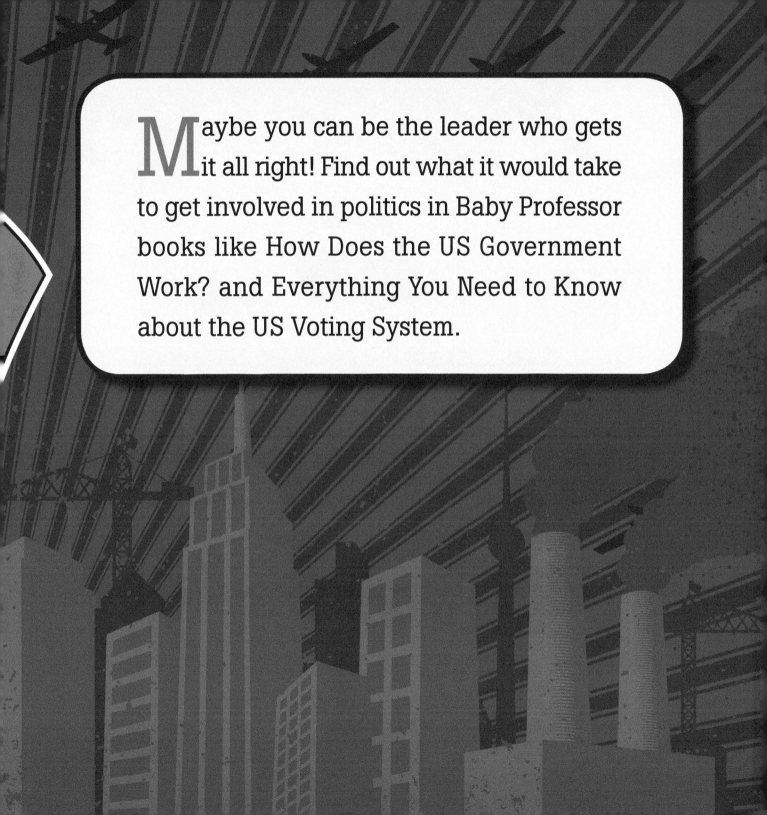

Maybe you can be the leader who gets it all right! Find out what it would take to get involved in politics in Baby Professor books like How Does the US Government Work? and Everything You Need to Know about the US Voting System.

Visit

BABY PROFESSOR
EDUCATION KIDS

www.BabyProfessorBooks.com

to download Free Baby Professor eBooks
and view our catalog of new and exciting
Children's Books

CPSIA information can be obtained
at www.ICGtesting.com
Printed in the USA
BVHW091543210921
617191BV00010B/668